Adapt ability

(Key Skills to Rising & Shining During Changing & Unforeseen Challenges!)

Gerard Assey

Adapt
ability

By

Gerard Assey

Published by:

Gerard Assey

19/18, Palli Arasan Street

Anna Nagar East

Chennai - 600 102

ISBN: 978-93-92492-47-1

Table of Contents

Preface

Welcome to **"Adaptability: *Key Skills to Rising & Shining During Changing & Unforeseen Challenges!"*** In a world that is constantly evolving, adaptability has become more than just a desirable trait – it is a vital skill that can determine our success in personal and professional spheres.

This book is a comprehensive guide to understanding and developing the essential skills needed to embrace change, navigate uncertainties, and thrive amidst unforeseen challenges. Whether you are an individual seeking personal growth, a professional striving for career advancement, or a leader guiding others through transformations, the concepts and strategies explored in this book will empower you to embrace adaptability and rise above the complexities of a rapidly changing world.

Through detailed insights, practical examples, and actionable advice, we will explore the psychology behind adaptability, the benefits it brings, and the skills required to cultivate it. From developing a growth mindset and building resilience to enhancing emotional intelligence and fostering flexibility, each chapter will delve into key aspects of adaptability and provide you with the tools to unlock your full potential.

Moreover, we will examine how to adapt to change both in the workplace and personal life. You will discover strategies for managing organizational changes, adapting to new roles and responsibilities, and thriving in dynamic work environments. Additionally, we will explore how to navigate major

life events, manage life transitions, and maintain well-being during times of change.
The journey towards adaptability is not a solitary one. It is a path that we walk together, supporting and inspiring one another. Throughout this book, you will find stories of individuals who have successfully embraced change and overcome challenges, as well as real-life examples of organizations that have pivoted and thrived in the face of uncertainty. These narratives serve as beacons of inspiration, illustrating the transformative power of adaptability in action.

It is my hope that **"Adaptability: *Key Skills to Rising & Shining During Changing & Unforeseen Challenges!*"** will serve as a roadmap for your personal and professional growth. By embracing adaptability, you will gain the confidence and resilience to navigate the ever-changing landscape of life. Together, let us embark on this transformative journey and embrace the challenges that lie ahead.

Remember, change is not something to fear but an opportunity for growth. With the right skills, mindset, and support, you can rise above any challenge and shine brightly in a world of endless possibilities.

Wishing you success and fulfillment on your path to adaptability!

Adaptability- Utmost Importance in a Rapidly Changing World

In today's rapidly changing world, adaptability has become a vital skill for individuals to navigate the unpredictable and dynamic nature of various aspects of life. Whether in personal or professional spheres, the ability to adapt to new circumstances, challenges, and opportunities is crucial for success and fulfillment.

The Importance of Adaptability in a Rapidly Changing World:

The world we live in is characterized by constant change and uncertainty. Technological advancements, economic fluctuations, and global events can significantly impact our lives. In such an environment, adaptability becomes essential to effectively respond to these changes and thrive in the face of adversity.

For instance, consider the impact of technological advancements on various industries. The rise of automation and artificial intelligence has disrupted traditional job roles and created new ones. Those who have embraced adaptability by up-skilling themselves and embracing emerging technologies have been able to stay relevant and even advance their careers. On the other hand, those who resisted change and failed to adapt have found themselves struggling to keep up or even rendered obsolete.

Similarly, in a globalized world, cultural diversity and globalization have brought about new challenges and opportunities. The ability to adapt to different cultures, customs, and work environments has become crucial for individuals and businesses operating in a global context. Those who can adapt their communication styles, embrace diverse perspectives, and navigate cultural differences effectively are more likely to succeed in international collaborations.

The Need for Adaptability in Personal and Professional Life:

Adaptability is not limited to professional settings; it is equally essential in our personal lives. Life presents us with unexpected events, major transitions, and unforeseen challenges. The ability to adapt helps us cope with these situations, maintain emotional well-being, and continue moving forward.

For example, consider a person who experiences a significant career setback, such as job loss. An individual with adaptability skills will approach this setback as an opportunity for growth, exploring new career paths, acquiring new skills, or even considering entrepreneurship. In contrast, someone lacking adaptability may become overwhelmed by the change, struggle to find alternative options, and experience prolonged unemployment.

In personal relationships, adaptability plays a crucial role in maintaining healthy connections. Life partners who can adapt to the changing needs and circumstances of each other are more likely to build long-lasting and fulfilling relationships. Parenting also requires adaptability, as children grow and develop, requiring adjustments in parenting styles and approaches.

In summary, adaptability is of utmost importance in a rapidly changing world. Whether it's adapting to technological advancements, global dynamics, unexpected events, or personal relationships, the ability to adapt allows individuals to thrive amidst uncertainty. By embracing adaptability, individuals can seize opportunities, overcome challenges, and lead fulfilling lives both personally and professionally.

Understanding Adaptability

Defining Adaptability and Its Significance:
Adaptability can be defined as the ability to adjust, change, or modify oneself in response to new circumstances, challenges, or opportunities. It involves being flexible, open-minded, and willing to embrace change. Adaptability is not merely about survival; it is about thriving and flourishing in the face of changing circumstances.

Significance of Adaptability:
Adaptability holds immense significance in various aspects of life. It enables individuals to:

- ✓ Navigate Change: In a world characterized by rapid change, those who can adapt are better equipped to navigate transitions, whether it's a change in technology, work environment, or personal circumstances. They can quickly adjust their mindset, skills, and strategies to align with the new reality.
- ✓ Seize Opportunities: Opportunities often arise unexpectedly, and being adaptable allows individuals to recognize and capitalize on them. Whether it's a new project at work, a chance encounter, or a sudden change in the market, adaptable individuals are ready to embrace these opportunities and make the most of them.
- ✓ Overcome Challenges: Challenges are an inevitable part of life. Being adaptable helps individuals face and overcome these challenges with resilience. They can assess

the situation, adjust their approach, and find innovative solutions.

- ✓ Embrace Innovation: Adaptability and innovation go hand in hand. In a rapidly evolving world, innovation drives progress. Those who are adaptable are more likely to embrace new ideas, experiment with novel approaches, and contribute to the advancement of their field.

The Psychology Behind Adaptability:

The psychology behind adaptability involves several cognitive and behavioral factors:

- ✓ Cognitive Flexibility: Adaptability is closely tied to cognitive flexibility, which refers to the ability to shift thinking, adapt to new information, and see situations from multiple perspectives. Cognitive flexibility allows individuals to let go of rigid thinking patterns and embrace alternative strategies.
- ✓ Growth Mindset: Having a growth mindset is crucial for adaptability. Individuals with a growth mindset believe that their abilities and intelligence can be developed through effort and learning. They see challenges as opportunities for growth rather than setbacks. This mindset fosters a willingness to learn, change, and adapt.
- ✓ Emotional Regulation: Emotional regulation plays a significant role in adaptability. Being able to manage emotions effectively helps individuals cope with stress, uncertainty, and setbacks. It allows them to stay focused, make rational decisions, and maintain a positive outlook even in challenging situations.

Benefits of Being Adaptable:

- ✓ Professional Success: In the workplace, adaptability is highly valued by employers. Adaptable individuals can quickly adapt to new technologies, processes, and roles. They are more likely to take on new challenges, show resilience in the face of setbacks, and exhibit a willingness to learn and grow. These qualities often lead to career advancement and professional success.

  For example, consider a marketing professional who embraces adaptability. They stay updated with the latest digital marketing trends, learn new tools and strategies, and adapt their approach to target changing consumer behaviors. As a result, they can drive successful campaigns, attract new customers, and stay ahead of competitors.

- ✓ Improved Relationships: Adaptability enhances relationships, both personal and professional. Being adaptable allows individuals to understand and accommodate others' needs, preferences, and perspectives. It fosters effective communication, collaboration, and empathy, leading to stronger connections and smoother interactions.

  For instance, a team leader who is adaptable recognizes the diverse strengths and working styles of team members. They create an environment that allows individuals to contribute their best, adapt to different work styles, and foster collaboration among team members.

- ✓ Enhanced Resilience and Well-being: Adaptable individuals are more resilient and better equipped to handle stressful situations. They bounce back from setbacks, find alternative solutions, and maintain a positive mindset. This resilience contributes to overall well-being, reducing stress levels and promoting mental and emotional health.

  For example, consider a student who faces a challenging academic environment. An adaptable student will assess their study methods, seek support, and adjust their approach to improve their performance. They maintain a growth mindset, focus on continuous learning, and experience reduced stress levels compared to someone who resists change and becomes overwhelmed by the difficulties.

In summary, adaptability is a key psychological trait that empowers individuals to navigate change, seize opportunities, overcome challenges, and embrace innovation. It is closely linked to cognitive flexibility, a growth mindset, and emotional regulation. Being adaptable brings numerous benefits, including professional success, improved relationships, and enhanced resilience and well-being.

Assessing Your Adaptability

Before we go any further, assessing one's adaptability can help provide insights into areas of strength and areas that may require further development. Here are a few questions to help you assess your adaptability:

- ✓ How do you typically respond to unexpected changes or disruptions in your plans? a) I become stressed and find it difficult to adapt. b) I feel a bit uneasy but can adjust my plans accordingly. c) I embrace the change and see it as an opportunity for growth.
- ✓ How comfortable are you with trying new things or stepping outside of your comfort zone? a) I prefer to stick to what I know and feel uncomfortable trying new things. b) I am willing to try new things but may feel hesitant or cautious. c) I actively seek out new experiences and enjoy stepping outside of my comfort zone.
- ✓ How do you approach challenges or setbacks in your life? a) I tend to get discouraged and may struggle to find alternative solutions. b) I am able to adapt and find solutions, but it takes some effort. c) I view challenges as opportunities for growth and easily find alternative solutions.
- ✓ How open are you to feedback and suggestions from others? a) I am resistant to feedback and prefer to stick to my own ideas. b) I am open to feedback but may feel defensive or resistant at times. c) I actively

seek feedback and value different perspectives to improve my ideas.

- ✓ How do you handle change in your work or personal life? a) I find it challenging to adapt to change and may feel overwhelmed. b) I can adapt to change but may require some time and effort to adjust. c) I embrace change and see it as an opportunity for growth and learning.
- ✓ How do you approach learning and acquiring new skills or knowledge? a) I prefer to stick to what I already know and am hesitant to learn new things. b) I am willing to learn new things, but it may take some time and effort. c) I actively seek out opportunities to learn and continuously expand my knowledge and skills.
- ✓ How well do you handle uncertainty or ambiguity? a) I struggle with uncertainty and feel the need for clear directions or answers. b) I can manage uncertainty to some extent but may feel uneasy or anxious. c) I embrace uncertainty and see it as an opportunity for creativity and innovation.

Scoring:

- ✓ Give yourself 1 point for each (a) response.
- ✓ Give yourself 2 points for each (b) response.
- ✓ Give yourself 3 points for each (c) response.

Interpretation:

- ✓ 7-10 points: You may have some room for growth in adaptability. Consider focusing on developing a growth mindset, embracing change, and seeking out new experiences.
- ✓ 11-15 points: You demonstrate moderate adaptability. Continue to build on your

strengths and work on areas that may require further development.

- ✓ 16-21 points: You exhibit a high level of adaptability. Congratulations! Your mindset and skills are well-aligned with embracing change and navigating challenges.

Remember that adaptability is a skill that can be developed and improved over time. Regardless of your score, with intention, practice, and a willingness to embrace change, you can enhance your adaptability and thrive in an ever-changing world.

Why is Adaptability Important: The Benefits

Adaptability is important for several reasons, as it offers numerous benefits in both personal and professional contexts. Here are some key benefits of adaptability, along with examples illustrating their significance:

1. Embracing Opportunities: Adaptability allows individuals to seize new opportunities that arise amidst change. For instance, imagine a professional who demonstrates adaptability by learning new skills and staying updated with industry trends. This adaptability enables them to take advantage of emerging job roles or advancements in their field, opening up new career prospects and growth opportunities.
2. Navigating Uncertainty: In a rapidly changing world, uncertainty is inevitable. Adaptability equips individuals with the ability to navigate uncertainty with confidence and resilience. Consider an entrepreneur who adapts their business model in response to market trends or a student who adjusts their study approach when faced with a challenging subject. By being adaptable, they can navigate uncertainties and maintain progress towards their goals.
3. Problem Solving and Innovation: Adaptability fosters creative problem-solving and innovation. When faced with unexpected challenges, adaptable individuals are more likely to think outside the box and explore alternative solutions. For example, a team

member who adapts their approach to a project based on changing client requirements may propose innovative solutions that lead to better outcomes.

4. Building Resilience: Adaptability and resilience go hand in hand. Being adaptable allows individuals to bounce back from setbacks and recover quickly from adversity. An individual who experiences a career setback but demonstrates adaptability can quickly reassess their skills and seek alternative employment opportunities, ultimately rebounding stronger and more determined.
5. Effective Collaboration: Adaptability enhances collaboration and teamwork. When individuals are open to new ideas and flexible in their approaches, they can work more effectively with diverse teams. For instance, in a multinational company, employees who are adaptable and open-minded are better able to understand and appreciate cultural differences, leading to improved collaboration and synergy among team members.
6. Personal Growth and Learning: Adaptability promotes personal growth and continuous learning. By embracing new challenges and being open to change, individuals expand their knowledge and skills, fostering personal and professional development. An individual who takes on challenging assignments or pursues new hobbies that require adaptability gains valuable experiences and broadens their perspectives.
7. Enhancing Well-being: Adaptability contributes to overall well-being by reducing stress and

enhancing resilience. When individuals are adaptable, they are better equipped to cope with change and manage the associated stressors. They can find balance in their personal and professional lives and maintain a positive outlook even in the face of challenges.

In summary, adaptability is important because it enables individuals to embrace opportunities, navigate uncertainty, solve problems creatively, build resilience, collaborate effectively, foster personal growth, and enhance well-being. By cultivating adaptability, individuals can thrive in an ever-changing world and lead fulfilling and successful lives.

The Consequences of a Lack of Adaptability

The consequences of a lack of adaptability can have a significant impact on individuals and organizations. Here are some consequences of lacking adaptability, along with examples that shed light on why some people struggle to adapt:

1. Missed Opportunities: Without adaptability, individuals may miss out on valuable opportunities for growth and success. For instance, imagine an employee who resists learning new technologies or refuses to adapt their skills to evolving market demands. As a result, they may miss out on promotions or career advancements that require adaptability, limiting their professional growth.
2. Stagnation and Obsolescence: In a rapidly changing world, lack of adaptability can lead to stagnation and obsolescence. For example, consider a business that fails to adapt its products or services to meet changing customer preferences. The company may lose its competitive edge and struggle to remain relevant in the market, ultimately facing declining sales and potential closure.
3. Increased Stress and Resilience Challenges: Without adaptability, individuals may experience higher levels of stress and struggle to cope with unexpected challenges. For instance, someone who is resistant to change may find themselves overwhelmed when faced with a sudden shift in work responsibilities or organizational restructuring.

The inability to adapt can lead to increased stress, reduced productivity, and difficulties in bouncing back from setbacks.

4. Strained Relationships and Collaboration: Lack of adaptability can strain relationships, both personal and professional. Individuals who resist new ideas or different perspectives may struggle to collaborate effectively with others. This can create conflicts, hinder teamwork, and limit the ability to find innovative solutions. For example, a team member who is rigid in their thinking may resist alternative approaches suggested by colleagues, causing tension and hindering progress.
5. Limited Personal Growth and Development: Those who lack adaptability may experience limited personal growth and development. When individuals are resistant to change, they may remain within their comfort zones, avoiding new experiences and learning opportunities. This can hinder their personal and professional growth and limit their ability to acquire new skills or explore different avenues for success.

Now, let's explore some reasons why some individuals struggle to adapt:

1. Fear of the Unknown: Change can be accompanied by uncertainty, and some people are naturally resistant to the unknown. Fear of the unfamiliar can lead individuals to cling to familiar routines and resist adapting to new situations or challenges.

2. Comfort Zones and Familiarity: Many people find comfort in routines and familiarity. Stepping outside of their comfort zones can be daunting, and they may prefer to stick with what they know, even if it limits their growth and potential.
3. Fixed Mindset: Individuals with a fixed mindset believe that their abilities and traits are fixed and unchangeable. They may resist adapting because they perceive it as a challenge to their self-concept. They may believe that their skills and capabilities are fixed, leading to resistance when confronted with the need to learn and grow.
4. Lack of Self-Awareness: Some individuals may lack self-awareness, making it difficult for them to recognize the need for adaptability. They may be unaware of their own limitations or resistant to feedback, hindering their ability to see the benefits of adapting.
5. Resistance to Change: Change can be uncomfortable and disrupt established routines. Some people naturally resist change, seeking stability and predictability. This resistance can make it challenging for them to adapt to new circumstances.

It is important to note that while some individuals may struggle to adapt, adaptability is a skill that can be developed and improved with practice, self-reflection, and a willingness to embrace change. Overcoming the consequences of a lack of adaptability starts with recognizing its importance and actively working towards developing a more adaptable mindset and approach.

Key Traits of an Adaptable Person

Key traits of an adaptable person include:

1. Open-mindedness: An adaptable person is open to new ideas, perspectives, and possibilities. They are receptive to change and willing to consider alternative approaches. For example, when faced with a different way of doing things at work, an adaptable person listens to their colleagues' suggestions with an open mind and is willing to give it a try.
2. Flexibility: Adaptable individuals are flexible in their thinking and behavior. They can adjust their plans and strategies as needed, without getting overly attached to a specific outcome. For instance, if a project timeline gets unexpectedly shortened, an adaptable person is willing to reorganize their priorities and adapt their work schedule accordingly.
3. Resilience: Adaptable individuals possess resilience, allowing them to bounce back from setbacks and challenges. They have the ability to recover quickly from adversity and continue moving forward. For example, if a business initiative fails, an adaptable entrepreneur assesses the situation, learns from it, and adjusts their approach to try again.
4. Curiosity and Learning Orientation: Adaptable individuals have a curiosity-driven mindset and a desire for continuous learning. They seek out new knowledge, skills, and experiences to expand their capabilities. For instance, an adaptable employee actively seeks opportunities to attend workshops,

seminars, and industry conferences to stay updated and acquire new skills relevant to their profession.

5. Self-awareness: Adaptable people possess a high level of self-awareness. They understand their strengths, weaknesses, and preferences, which allows them to identify areas where adaptation is needed. For example, an adaptable leader recognizes their own resistance to change and actively works on developing a more flexible approach.
6. Problem-solving skills: Adaptable individuals excel in problem-solving. They are skilled at analyzing situations, identifying alternative solutions, and making informed decisions. For example, when faced with a challenging customer request, an adaptable customer service representative thinks creatively to find a solution that meets the customer's needs within the company's policies.
7. Emotional intelligence: Adaptable individuals have a strong sense of emotional intelligence. They are aware of their own emotions and can effectively manage them. Additionally, they are attuned to the emotions of others, which helps them navigate relationships and collaborate effectively during times of change. For instance, an adaptable team member understands the anxieties and concerns of their colleagues during a period of organizational restructuring and provides support and empathy.
8. Proactive mindset: Adaptable individuals possess a proactive mindset. They are not passive observers but actively anticipate and

prepare for change. They seek out opportunities to grow and develop, rather than waiting for change to happen to them. For example, an adaptable entrepreneur continuously scans the market, identifies emerging trends, and proactively adjusts their business strategy to stay ahead of the competition.

Overall, an adaptable person combines open-mindedness, flexibility, resilience, curiosity, self-awareness, problem-solving skills, emotional intelligence, and a proactive mindset. These traits enable them to navigate changing circumstances, embrace new challenges, and thrive in an ever-evolving world.

The Key Skills of Adaptability

Key skills of adaptability include:

1. Flexibility: Flexibility is the ability to adjust to changing circumstances and embrace new approaches. It involves being open to different ideas, perspectives, and methods. For example, if a project's requirements change, an adaptable individual can modify their plans and adapt their work accordingly.
2. Problem-solving: Adaptability requires strong problem-solving skills. It involves the ability to analyze complex situations, identify potential obstacles or challenges, and develop effective solutions. For instance, when faced with a sudden change in market demand, an adaptable business owner can quickly assess the situation, identify new target markets, and adjust their marketing strategies accordingly.
3. Resilience: Resilience is the capacity to bounce back from setbacks and persevere in the face of adversity. It involves maintaining a positive mindset, managing stress, and adapting to unexpected challenges. For example, an adaptable employee who faces a layoff can quickly regroup, update their resume, and explore new job opportunities.
4. Emotional intelligence: Emotional intelligence is the ability to recognize and manage emotions, both in oneself and others. It involves self-awareness, empathy, and effective communication. An adaptable individual with high emotional intelligence can navigate interpersonal dynamics, understand

and address the concerns of team members during times of change, and build strong relationships.

5. Continuous learning: Adaptability requires a commitment to continuous learning and personal growth. It involves seeking out new knowledge, acquiring new skills, and staying updated with industry trends. For instance, an adaptable professional attends workshops, takes online courses, or reads relevant books to enhance their expertise and adapt to changing job requirements.
6. Decision-making: Effective decision-making is crucial for adaptability. It involves evaluating different options, considering potential outcomes, and making informed choices. An adaptable individual can make decisions swiftly and confidently, even in uncertain or ambiguous situations. For example, a manager who needs to make quick decisions regarding resource allocation during a company-wide restructuring demonstrates adaptability by considering various factors and making timely decisions.
7. Collaboration: Adaptability also involves the ability to collaborate effectively with others. It requires strong communication skills, active listening, and a willingness to work as part of a team. For instance, an adaptable team member can adjust their working style to accommodate diverse perspectives and contribute to collective problem-solving during a project that undergoes changes.
8. Creativity and innovation: Adaptability goes hand in hand with creativity and innovation. It

involves thinking outside the box, exploring new ideas, and embracing experimentation. For example, an adaptable entrepreneur continually looks for innovative ways to improve their products or services, staying ahead of competitors and meeting evolving customer needs.

By developing and honing these key skills of adaptability, individuals can thrive in uncertain and changing environments, seize opportunities, overcome challenges, and continuously grow both personally and professionally.

Improving the Skills of Adaptability

To improve your skills of adaptability, here are some steps you can take:

1. Embrace Change: Embrace change as an opportunity for growth and development. Seek out new experiences and challenges that push you outside your comfort zone. For example, take on new projects at work that require you to learn new skills or volunteer for roles that expose you to unfamiliar situations.
2. Foster a Growth Mindset: Adopt a growth mindset, believing that you can develop and improve your abilities through effort and learning. Emphasize the process of learning rather than focusing solely on outcomes. For instance, if you face a setback, approach it with curiosity and a desire to learn from the experience rather than viewing it as a failure.
3. Seek Diverse Perspectives: Actively seek out diverse perspectives and opinions. Engage in discussions with people from different backgrounds, industries, or disciplines. This exposure to diverse viewpoints broadens your thinking and helps you consider alternative approaches. For example, join networking events, attend conferences, or participate in online forums to connect with individuals outside your immediate circle.
4. Practice Flexibility: Practice flexibility in your thinking and actions. Be open to new ideas, methods, and approaches. Challenge your own assumptions and be willing to adapt your plans when necessary. For instance, if a

project takes an unexpected turn, instead of resisting, adjust your plans and seek creative solutions.

5. Learn Continuously: Develop a thirst for learning and commit to continuous personal and professional development. Seek out opportunities to acquire new knowledge, skills, and experiences. Engage in activities like reading books, taking online courses, attending workshops, or participating in training programs. For example, if you want to improve your digital marketing skills, enroll in an online course or join a marketing webinar series.
6. Build Resilience: Cultivate resilience, which helps you bounce back from setbacks and challenges. Develop coping mechanisms to manage stress and maintain a positive mindset. Seek support from mentors, friends, or support groups during difficult times. For instance, practice mindfulness or engage in physical activities that promote resilience and well-being.
7. Emphasize Problem-Solving: Enhance your problem-solving skills by practicing structured approaches to problem-solving. Break down complex problems into smaller, manageable parts, and systematically analyze and evaluate potential solutions. Experiment with different strategies and learn from both successes and failures. For example, when faced with a difficult decision, use techniques such as SWOT analysis or decision matrices to weigh different options and make informed choices.

8. Embrace New Technologies: Stay up-to-date with technological advancements and embrace new tools and technologies that can enhance your productivity and efficiency. Adapt to new digital platforms, software, or automation tools that are relevant to your field. For example, if your organization adopts a new project management software, invest time in learning its features and functionalities.

By implementing these steps and actively working on improving your adaptability skills, you can become more agile, resilient, and effective in navigating changing circumstances and seizing opportunities for growth and success.

Key Ingredients for an Adaptive Thinking Mindset

Key ingredients for an adaptive thinking mindset include:

1. Curiosity: A curious mindset fuels adaptive thinking. It involves a natural inclination to explore, ask questions, and seek out new knowledge. Curiosity encourages individuals to challenge assumptions, explore different perspectives, and consider alternative solutions. For example, an adaptive thinker in a business setting might proactively research emerging trends, explore new markets, and ask critical questions to uncover innovative opportunities.
2. Open-mindedness: Open-mindedness is essential for adaptive thinking. It involves being receptive to new ideas, perspectives, and feedback. Open-minded individuals are willing to consider different viewpoints, even if they initially seem contrary to their own beliefs. For instance, an open-minded leader listens attentively to diverse input from team members, considering various approaches before making decisions.
3. Critical Thinking: Critical thinking involves analyzing information, evaluating evidence, and making reasoned judgments. Adaptive thinkers critically assess situations, weigh pros and cons, and consider potential consequences before taking action. They are skilled at recognizing patterns, identifying assumptions, and questioning the validity of

assumptions. For example, an adaptive thinker in a problem-solving scenario may critically analyze data, challenge existing assumptions, and propose innovative solutions.

4. Flexibility: Flexibility is a key ingredient of adaptive thinking. It involves the ability to adapt and adjust plans, strategies, and perspectives in response to changing circumstances. Flexible thinkers embrace uncertainty and are willing to change course when necessary. For instance, a flexible thinker in project management is open to adjusting timelines, reallocating resources, and adapting project scope to accommodate evolving priorities.
5. Optimism and Resilience: Optimism and resilience are important for maintaining an adaptive thinking mindset. Optimistic individuals approach challenges with a positive outlook, believing in their ability to overcome obstacles. They bounce back from setbacks, learn from failures, and remain motivated in the face of adversity. For example, an optimistically resilient thinker who experiences a setback in their career sees it as an opportunity for growth, learns from the experience, and adapts their approach for future success.
6. Systems Thinking: Adaptive thinkers employ systems thinking, which involves understanding the interconnectedness and interdependencies of various elements within a system. They consider the broader context, anticipate ripple effects, and recognize how

changes in one area can impact other parts of the system. For instance, a systems thinker in business understands how changes in customer preferences can affect product development, marketing strategies, and supply chain management.

7. Continuous Learning: Adaptive thinkers have a thirst for continuous learning. They actively seek out new knowledge, stay updated with industry trends, and engage in ongoing personal and professional development. They recognize that learning is a lifelong journey and embrace opportunities for growth. For example, an adaptive thinker attends conferences, workshops, and webinars to gain new insights, skills, and perspectives.

By cultivating these key ingredients of an adaptive thinking mindset, individuals can enhance their ability to navigate uncertainty, solve complex problems, and adapt to changing circumstances effectively. Adaptive thinking promotes creativity, innovation, and strategic decision-making, enabling individuals to thrive in dynamic and ever-evolving environments.

Developing a Growth Mindset

The Power of Mindset in Embracing Change:

Our mindset, or the way we perceive and interpret the world, plays a significant role in our ability to embrace change. A mindset that is open, flexible, and growth-oriented allows individuals to see change as an opportunity for growth and development. On the other hand, a fixed mindset, which believes that abilities are fixed and unchangeable, can hinder adaptability.

By cultivating a growth mindset, individuals can harness the power of their thoughts and beliefs to approach change with enthusiasm and resilience. They understand that their abilities can be developed through effort, learning, and experience. This mindset empowers them to see change as a chance to learn new skills, gain valuable experiences, and discover new possibilities.

Overcoming Resistance to Change:

Resistance to change is a natural response that can hinder adaptability. People often feel comfortable in familiar routines and environments, and the unknown can be intimidating. However, overcoming resistance to change is crucial for adaptability.

To overcome resistance, it is important to acknowledge and address the fears and concerns that arise. By reframing change as an opportunity rather than a threat, individuals can shift their perspective and embrace the possibilities that lie ahead. They can focus on the potential benefits and growth that change can bring, rather than dwelling on the uncertainties.

Additionally, breaking down the change into smaller, manageable steps can make it less overwhelming. By setting realistic goals and milestones, individuals can gradually adapt to the new situation, gaining confidence and reducing resistance along the way.

Cultivating a Growth Mindset for Adaptability:
Cultivating a growth mindset is essential for adaptability. Here are some strategies to develop and strengthen a growth mindset:

- ✓ Embrace Challenges: Instead of shying away from challenges, view them as opportunities for growth. Approach them with enthusiasm and a willingness to learn. When faced with a difficult task or situation, remind yourself that it is a chance to develop new skills and expand your capabilities.
  For example, imagine an employee who is assigned to lead a complex project that involves new technologies and requires collaborating with cross-functional teams. Instead of feeling overwhelmed, they embrace the challenge, seeing it as an opportunity to develop their leadership, technical, and teamwork skills.
- ✓ Emphasize Effort and Learning: Focus on the process of learning and improvement rather than solely on the end result. Recognize that effort, perseverance, and continuous learning are the keys to growth. Celebrate progress and small achievements along the way, acknowledging that setbacks are opportunities for learning and refinement.
  For instance, a student who receives a lower grade on an exam can view it as feedback for

improvement. They analyze their mistakes, seek additional resources or guidance, and put in extra effort to enhance their understanding of the subject matter.

- ✓ Embrace Failure as a Learning Opportunity: Shift your perspective on failure. Rather than seeing it as a reflection of your abilities, view it as a valuable learning experience. Embrace the lessons it offers and use them to refine your approach and make better decisions in the future. Failure is not a permanent setback but a stepping stone towards growth and improvement.

  For example, an entrepreneur who experiences a business venture that doesn't succeed can reflect on the lessons learned. They identify areas for improvement, adjust their strategies, and approach their next venture with newfound knowledge and resilience.

- ✓ Seek Feedback and Collaboration: Embrace feedback as a tool for growth. Be open to constructive criticism and use it to identify areas of improvement. Surround yourself with supportive individuals who can provide different perspectives and challenge your thinking. Collaborating with others fosters continuous learning and helps to expand your knowledge and adaptability.

  For instance, a team member who actively seeks feedback from colleagues and superiors can gather insights and suggestions for improving their work. They collaborate with others, valuing diverse perspectives, and adapt their approaches based on the feedback received.

In summary, developing a growth mindset is crucial for adaptability. It involves embracing challenges, overcoming resistance to change, and cultivating a mindset focused on effort, learning, and embracing failure as a learning opportunity. By adopting a growth mindset, individuals can navigate change with resilience, continuously improve their skills, and thrive in dynamic environments.

Building Resilience

Understanding Resilience and Its Connection to Adaptability:

Resilience can be defined as the ability to recover, adapt, and bounce back from adversity, setbacks, or challenges. It is closely linked to adaptability, as both concepts involve navigating through difficult circumstances and emerging stronger on the other side.

Resilience enables individuals to maintain a positive mindset, effectively manage stress, and continue moving forward despite obstacles. It involves cultivating inner strength, emotional well-being, and the ability to cope with and learn from difficult experiences.

Strategies for Building Resilience:

1. Cultivate Self-Awareness: Building resilience starts with self-awareness. Understand your emotions, thoughts, and reactions to stressors. Recognize your strengths, values, and coping mechanisms. Self-awareness allows you to identify areas for growth and develop strategies to handle challenges effectively.
2. Foster a Supportive Network: Surround yourself with a supportive network of friends, family, mentors, and colleagues. These individuals can provide emotional support, guidance, and different perspectives. They can offer encouragement during tough times and help you see new possibilities and solutions.

3. Practice Positive Thinking: Foster a positive mindset by focusing on gratitude, optimism, and self-belief. Replace negative thoughts with positive affirmations. Develop a habit of reframing challenges as opportunities for growth. Positive thinking enhances resilience by maintaining a hopeful outlook and building confidence in your ability to overcome difficulties.
4. Develop Coping Strategies: Identify healthy coping strategies that work for you. These can include physical activities, mindfulness, journaling, meditation, or engaging in hobbies. Experiment with different techniques and find what helps you manage stress and maintain emotional well-being during challenging times.
5. Embrace Adaptability: Resilience is closely tied to adaptability. Embrace change and uncertainty as opportunities for growth. Develop flexibility and a willingness to adjust your plans and strategies when needed. Being adaptable allows you to navigate unexpected situations and find alternative paths forward.

Overcoming Setbacks and Bouncing Back Stronger:

- ✓ Learn from Failure: View setbacks and failures as learning experiences. Analyze what went wrong and identify lessons that can be applied in the future. Use failure as a stepping stone to refine your strategies, improve your skills, and gain valuable insights.

  For example, an athlete who fails to achieve their desired performance in a competition can analyze their training methods, seek feedback from coaches, and make adjustments to enhance their performance in future competitions.

- ✓ Practice Self-Compassion: Be kind to yourself when facing setbacks. Avoid self-blame or harsh criticism. Instead, practice self-compassion by acknowledging that setbacks are a natural part of life and that everyone experiences them. Treat yourself with understanding, forgiveness, and patience as you navigate challenges.
- ✓ Set Realistic Goals: When bouncing back from setbacks, set realistic goals that allow for gradual progress. Break down larger goals into smaller, achievable steps. Celebrate small victories along the way to maintain motivation and build momentum towards success.

  For instance, a business owner who experiences a setback, such as a product launch that didn't meet expectations, can set smaller, achievable goals to improve the product, refine marketing strategies, and re-engage with customers.
- ✓ Seek Support and Feedback: Reach out for support during challenging times. Share your experiences with trusted individuals who can provide guidance, encouragement, and constructive feedback. Collaborate with mentors or professionals in your field who can offer valuable insights and advice.

In summary, building resilience involves understanding its connection to adaptability, implementing strategies to foster resilience, and overcoming setbacks with strength and determination. By cultivating self-awareness, developing coping strategies, embracing adaptability, and seeking support, individuals can bounce back from adversity and navigate challenges with resilience and growth.

Tips to Enhance your Resilience

To enhance resilience, here are some ways and steps that can be taken:

1. Cultivate a Positive Mindset: Foster a positive outlook by focusing on opportunities and solutions rather than dwelling on problems. Practice gratitude, optimism, and self-compassion. For example, instead of viewing a setback as a failure, reframe it as a learning experience and identify the lessons you can take away from it.
2. Build Strong Support Networks: Surround yourself with supportive and positive individuals who can provide emotional support and encouragement during challenging times. Seek out mentors, friends, or support groups who can offer guidance and understanding. For instance, joining a professional network or participating in a hobby group can provide a sense of belonging and support.
3. Practice Self-Care: Prioritize self-care activities that promote physical, mental, and emotional well-being. Engage in regular exercise, get enough sleep, eat a balanced diet, and engage in activities that bring you joy and relaxation. Taking care of yourself strengthens your resilience and ability to cope with stress. For example, incorporating mindfulness or meditation into your daily routine can help reduce stress and promote emotional resilience.
4. Develop Problem-Solving Skills: Enhancing your problem-solving skills equips you with the

ability to face challenges head-on and find effective solutions. Break down problems into manageable steps, brainstorm alternative approaches, and seek input from others. For instance, if you encounter a work-related challenge, you can use techniques like the "5 Whys" to identify the root cause and develop strategies for addressing it.

5. Embrace Change and Adaptability: Resilient individuals embrace change as an opportunity for growth rather than fearing it. They adapt to new situations, remain flexible, and seek out opportunities for learning and development. For example, if you are faced with a major life change such as a career transition, approach it with a growth mindset, explore new possibilities, and view it as a chance to pursue new passions.
6. Practice Stress Management Techniques: Develop healthy coping mechanisms to manage stress effectively. Engage in activities such as deep breathing exercises, meditation, journaling, or engaging in hobbies that help you relax and recharge. These techniques help build resilience by reducing the negative impact of stress on your mental and physical well-being.
7. Learn from Failure and Setbacks: Resilient individuals view failures and setbacks as learning opportunities. Instead of dwelling on past mistakes, they reflect on what went wrong, identify lessons learned, and use that knowledge to adapt and improve. For example, if a business venture doesn't succeed, resilient entrepreneurs analyze the

factors that contributed to the failure, adjust their strategies, and apply the newfound knowledge in their next endeavor.

8. Develop a Growth Mindset: Embrace a growth mindset, which involves believing in your ability to grow, learn, and develop through effort and perseverance. View challenges as opportunities for personal growth rather than fixed limitations. For instance, if you receive constructive criticism, see it as a chance to improve rather than taking it as a personal attack.

Remember that building resilience is a gradual process. By implementing these steps and incorporating resilience-building practices into your daily life, you can cultivate a stronger sense of resilience and effectively navigate challenges and adversity.

Enhancing Emotional Intelligence

The Role of Emotional Intelligence in Adaptability:

Emotional intelligence (EI) refers to the ability to understand and manage one's own emotions and effectively navigate interpersonal relationships. It plays a crucial role in adaptability by enhancing self-awareness, self-regulation, social awareness, and relationship management skills.

Individuals with high emotional intelligence can better understand and regulate their emotions, adapt their behavior to different situations, and navigate change and uncertainty with resilience. They also excel in building positive relationships and effectively collaborating with others, which is essential for adaptability in personal and professional contexts.

Developing Self-Awareness and Self-Regulation:

- ✓ Self-Awareness: Self-awareness is the foundation of emotional intelligence. It involves recognizing and understanding one's own emotions, strengths, weaknesses, values, and motivations. Developing self-awareness allows individuals to accurately assess their emotions, reactions, and thought patterns in different situations.

  For example, a leader with high self-awareness can recognize when they feel overwhelmed or stressed in a fast-paced work environment. They understand their triggers and take proactive steps to manage their stress levels, such as practicing mindfulness or delegating tasks.

- ✓ Self-Regulation: Self-regulation refers to the ability to manage and control one's emotions, impulses, and behaviors. It involves maintaining emotional balance, adapting to change, and exercising self-discipline. Self-regulation allows individuals to respond thoughtfully and appropriately to challenges, rather than reacting impulsively.

  For instance, an employee who receives critical feedback from their supervisor can regulate their initial defensive reaction and instead respond with openness and a willingness to learn. They can reflect on the feedback, manage their emotions, and take constructive steps to improve their performance.

Improving Social Awareness and Relationship Management:

- ✓ Social Awareness: Social awareness involves perceiving and understanding the emotions, needs, and perspectives of others. It includes empathy, the ability to put oneself in others' shoes and understand their experiences and feelings. Developing social awareness allows individuals to effectively navigate social dynamics, build rapport, and foster positive relationships.

  For example, a salesperson with high social awareness can accurately read their clients' emotions and respond appropriately. They can sense when a client is hesitant or excited and adjust their approach to build trust and meet the client's needs.

- ✓ Relationship Management: Relationship management involves effectively communicating, influencing, and building positive connections with others. It includes skills such as conflict resolution, teamwork, and collaboration. Individuals with strong relationship management skills can navigate interpersonal dynamics, resolve conflicts constructively, and foster cooperation among team members.

  For instance, a project manager with strong relationship management skills can bring together a diverse team, manage conflicts that arise during the project, and create an environment of collaboration and mutual respect. They understand the strengths and motivations of team members and leverage them to achieve project goals.

In summary, enhancing emotional intelligence is crucial for adaptability. By developing self-awareness and self-regulation, individuals can understand and manage their own emotions effectively. Improving social awareness and relationship management skills allows individuals to understand others, build positive connections, and navigate interpersonal dynamics. Embracing emotional intelligence empowers individuals to adapt to change, manage challenges, and foster positive relationships, contributing to their overall adaptability and success.

Flexibility and Open-Mindedness

Embracing Flexibility as a Key Skill for Adaptability:

Flexibility is a critical skill for adaptability as it involves being open to change, adjusting plans and strategies, and embracing new approaches. It allows individuals to navigate through uncertainties and challenges with agility and resilience.

Embracing flexibility means being willing to let go of preconceived notions, adapting to new circumstances, and embracing alternative solutions. It enables individuals to respond effectively to unexpected situations and seize opportunities for growth and innovation.

Letting Go of Rigid Thinking Patterns:

- ✓ Recognize Assumptions: Rigid thinking often stems from unconscious assumptions or beliefs. Recognizing and challenging these assumptions is the first step towards embracing flexibility. Question your own beliefs and consider alternative perspectives.

  For example, a manager who believes that remote work is less productive may hold rigid thinking patterns. By challenging this assumption and examining the evidence for both remote and in-person work, the manager may discover that remote work can indeed be productive and flexible.
- ✓ Embrace Uncertainty: Embracing flexibility requires embracing uncertainty. Instead of resisting or fearing the unknown, cultivate a mindset that views uncertainty as an

opportunity for growth and learning. Embrace ambiguity and be open to exploring new possibilities.

For instance, an entrepreneur launching a new business in a rapidly changing market must be willing to adapt their business model and strategies based on evolving customer needs and market dynamics. Embracing uncertainty allows them to remain agile and adjust their approach to stay relevant.

Embracing New Perspectives and Ideas:

- ✓ Seek Diverse Input: Actively seek out diverse perspectives and opinions. Engage with individuals from different backgrounds, cultures, and disciplines. By exposing yourself to diverse viewpoints, you broaden your understanding and challenge your own assumptions.

  For example, a team leader seeking input on a new project can invite team members from different departments or teams to contribute their ideas. By embracing diverse perspectives, the leader opens the door to innovative solutions and fosters a culture of open-mindedness.
- ✓ Foster a Learning Mindset: Cultivate a mindset of continuous learning and growth. Be open to new ideas and experiences. Instead of clinging to what you already know, approach each situation with a sense of curiosity and a willingness to learn from others.

  For instance, a student entering a new academic program can embrace a learning mindset by being open to new concepts and approaches. They actively engage with their peers and professors, seeking different perspectives and insights to broaden their knowledge.

- ✓ Embrace Feedback: Welcome feedback as an opportunity for growth. Instead of becoming defensive or dismissing feedback, consider it as a valuable source of information and improvement. Actively seek feedback from colleagues, mentors, or supervisors to gain different viewpoints and refine your ideas.

  For example, a writer who receives feedback on their work can view it as an opportunity to enhance their writing skills. They embrace the feedback, consider different suggestions, and incorporate them into their revisions.

In summary, flexibility and open-mindedness are vital for adaptability. Embracing flexibility involves letting go of rigid thinking patterns, being open to change, and adapting to new circumstances. Embracing new perspectives and ideas requires seeking diverse input, fostering a learning mindset, and embracing feedback. By embracing flexibility and open-mindedness, individuals can navigate change, discover innovative solutions, and thrive in dynamic environments.

The Importance of Continuous Learning

Continuous learning is crucial in today's rapidly evolving world. It is the process of acquiring new knowledge, skills, and competencies throughout one's life. Cultivating learning agility is essential for adaptability as it enables individuals to stay relevant, embrace change, and thrive in dynamic environments.

Continuous learning allows individuals to enhance their problem-solving abilities, adapt to new technologies and industry trends, and remain competitive in their personal and professional lives. It fosters a mindset of growth and improvement, enabling individuals to navigate through uncertainties and capitalize on new opportunities.

Developing a Thirst for Knowledge and Growth:

- ✓ Curiosity and Inquisitiveness: Cultivate a sense of curiosity and inquisitiveness about the world around you. Be eager to explore new ideas, concepts, and perspectives. Ask questions and seek answers. By nurturing a curious mindset, you ignite a passion for learning and growth.

  For example, an entrepreneur who wants to expand their business in a new market can cultivate curiosity by conducting market research, engaging with potential customers, and immersing themselves in the culture and dynamics of the target market.
- ✓ Embrace a Growth Mindset: Adopt a growth mindset, which is the belief that abilities and

intelligence can be developed through dedication and effort. Embrace challenges, view failures as learning opportunities, and maintain a positive attitude towards growth and improvement.

For instance, a software developer with a growth mindset approaches new programming languages or frameworks with enthusiasm, knowing that every learning experience contributes to their professional growth and expertise.

Strategies for Expanding Your Skill Set:

- ✓ Set Learning Goals: Define specific learning goals that align with your personal or professional aspirations. Break them down into smaller, manageable steps. By setting clear objectives, you create a roadmap for acquiring new skills and knowledge.

  For example, an individual aspiring to become a project manager can set a learning goal of obtaining a project management certification. They can outline the required courses, study materials, and timelines to achieve their objective.
- ✓ Pursue Formal and Informal Learning Opportunities: Actively seek out formal learning opportunities such as courses, workshops, or certifications. Engage in industry conferences or webinars that provide insights into emerging trends. Additionally, take advantage of informal learning opportunities like reading books, listening to podcasts, or participating in online

communities where you can exchange knowledge and ideas.

For instance, a marketing professional interested in enhancing their digital marketing skills can enroll in a specialized digital marketing course, attend industry conferences on the subject, and join online forums to learn from experts and practitioners.

- ✓ Seek Feedback and Mentoring: Seek feedback from mentors, colleagues, or subject matter experts to gain insights into areas for improvement and growth. Embrace constructive criticism and use it to refine your skills. Mentors can provide guidance, share their experiences, and offer valuable advice.

  For example, a young professional seeking to enhance their leadership skills can seek out a mentor who has a successful track record in leadership roles. The mentor can provide guidance, share leadership strategies, and offer feedback on their progress.

- ✓ Embrace New Experiences and Challenges: Step out of your comfort zone and embrace new experiences and challenges. Take on projects or assignments that push your boundaries and require you to acquire new skills. Embracing challenges fosters personal and professional growth.

  For instance, an engineer transitioning to a managerial role can take on a project that involves leading a cross-functional team. Although it may be outside their comfort zone, it provides an opportunity to develop skills in team management, communication, and conflict resolution.

In summary, cultivating learning agility is vital for adaptability. Continuous learning expands knowledge, enhances skills, and fosters a growth mindset. By developing a thirst for knowledge, setting learning goals, pursuing formal and informal learning opportunities, seeking feedback, and embracing new experiences, individuals can cultivate learning agility and thrive in a rapidly changing world.

Adapting to Change in the Workplace

Navigating Organizational Changes:

- ✓ Embrace a Positive Mindset: Adopting a positive mindset is crucial when navigating organizational changes. Instead of viewing change as a threat, see it as an opportunity for growth and development. Embrace the notion that change brings new possibilities and can lead to positive outcomes.

  For example, when a company undergoes a restructuring, an employee with a positive mindset approaches the situation with optimism. They recognize that the change may offer new career opportunities, increased responsibilities, or a chance to work with different teams.
- ✓ Stay Informed: Stay updated about organizational changes by actively seeking information from reliable sources. Attend company meetings, read internal communications, and engage in conversations with colleagues and superiors. Understanding the reasons behind the change and its impact on your role and the organization will help you adapt more effectively.

  For instance, during a merger or acquisition, an employee actively seeks information about the new structure, leadership, and strategic goals. This proactive approach allows them to align their work and goals with the new organizational direction.

Strategies for Adapting to New Roles and Responsibilities:

- ✓ Assess and Develop Skills: Evaluate the skills and competencies required for your new role and identify any gaps. Take proactive steps to develop or enhance those skills through training programs, workshops, or seeking mentorship. Continuously seek opportunities to learn and grow in your new role.

  For example, if you are transitioning from an individual contributor role to a managerial position, you may need to develop skills such as team leadership, delegation, and conflict resolution. Seek training or mentorship opportunities that focus on these areas.
- ✓ Seek Support and Build Relationships: Reach out to colleagues, supervisors, or mentors who can provide guidance and support during the transition. Building relationships with coworkers in your new team or department can help you quickly adapt to the new work environment and foster collaboration.

  For instance, if you join a new project team, take the initiative to introduce yourself to team members, attend team meetings, and actively contribute your ideas and insights. Building positive relationships establishes a foundation for effective collaboration and integration.

Thriving in a Dynamic Work Environment:

- ✓ Adaptability and Flexibility: Cultivate adaptability and flexibility as core attributes in a dynamic work environment. Be open to change, readily adjust to shifting priorities, and embrace new responsibilities. Approach challenges with a problem-solving mindset and seek innovative solutions.

For example, if a project deadline is moved up, an adaptable employee remains calm, reorganizes their priorities, and collaborates with team members to meet the new deadline.

- ✓ Continuous Learning: Stay updated with industry trends, advancements, and best practices. Seek opportunities to expand your knowledge and skills through training, conferences, or self-directed learning. Being proactive in your learning journey enables you to bring fresh insights and ideas to your work.

  For instance, in a rapidly evolving field like technology, a software developer actively pursues professional development opportunities to stay current with emerging technologies and methodologies.
- ✓ Resilience and Problem-Solving: Develop resilience to bounce back from setbacks and challenges. Maintain a solution-oriented mindset and focus on finding creative solutions to problems. Seek support when needed, leverage your strengths, and persevere in the face of adversity.

  For example, if a major project encounters unexpected obstacles, a resilient employee seeks input from team members, explores alternative approaches, and adapts their strategy to overcome the challenges.

In summary, adapting to change in the workplace requires a positive mindset, staying informed about organizational changes, and being proactive in developing the necessary skills. Strategies for adapting to new roles and responsibilities involve assessing skills, seeking support, and building relationships. Thriving in a dynamic work environment entails cultivating adaptability, continuous learning, resilience, and problem-solving abilities. By employing these strategies, individuals can navigate organizational changes and excel in their evolving roles.

Adapting to Personal Life Changes

Managing Life Transitions with Grace and Resilience:

- ✓ Acknowledge and Accept Change: The first step in adapting to personal life changes is acknowledging and accepting that change is a natural part of life. Recognize that transitions bring opportunities for growth, self-discovery, and new beginnings. Embrace the change with an open mind and a positive attitude.
  For example, when facing a job loss, an individual can acknowledge the situation, accept the reality, and view it as an opportunity to explore new career paths or pursue their passion.
- ✓ Practice Self-Reflection: Engage in self-reflection to gain clarity about your values, goals, and priorities. Reflect on how the life change aligns or conflicts with your personal aspirations. Understanding your own needs and desires will help you make informed decisions and navigate the transition effectively.
  For instance, when considering a major life change such as starting a family, individuals can reflect on their readiness, values, and long-term goals to make a well-informed decision.

Strategies for Adapting to Major Life Events:

- ✓ Seek Support: During times of major life events, reaching out for support is crucial. Lean on your social network, including family, friends, or support groups. Share your thoughts, concerns, and emotions with trusted individuals who can provide guidance, comfort, and practical assistance.

For example, when going through a divorce, seeking the support of a therapist or joining a divorce support group can provide emotional support and valuable insights from others who have experienced similar situations.

- ✓ Set Realistic Expectations: Adjusting to major life changes often requires setting realistic expectations. Recognize that transitions take time and may involve challenges along the way. Be patient with yourself and others involved in the process. Focus on progress rather than perfection.

  For instance, when relocating to a new city, it is important to set realistic expectations about the time it takes to adjust, build new social connections, and feel a sense of belonging in the new environment.

Maintaining Well-being During Times of Change:

- ✓ Self-Care and Stress Management: Prioritize self-care activities that promote physical, mental, and emotional well-being. Engage in regular exercise, practice mindfulness or meditation, maintain a balanced diet, and get sufficient rest. Implement stress management techniques such as deep breathing exercises or journaling to reduce anxiety and promote resilience.

  For example, during a career transition, engaging in regular exercise can help manage stress levels and improve overall well-being, while mindfulness practices can enhance focus and clarity during the decision-making process.

- ✓ Foster a Growth Mindset: Cultivate a growth mindset by viewing personal life changes as opportunities for personal growth, learning, and self-improvement. Embrace challenges and setbacks as learning experiences that can lead to personal development and resilience.

  For instance, when facing a health crisis, adopting a growth mindset can involve seeking information about the condition, exploring treatment options, and focusing on personal well-being to navigate the situation with strength and resilience.
- ✓ Adaptability and Flexibility: Embrace adaptability and flexibility as essential qualities during personal life changes. Be open to exploring new possibilities, adjusting plans when needed, and finding creative solutions to challenges that arise.

  For example, when becoming an empty nester, individuals can embrace the opportunity to rediscover their own interests, pursue new hobbies, or explore different paths in their personal lives.

In summary, adapting to personal life changes requires managing transitions with grace and resilience, implementing strategies to navigate major life events, and prioritizing well-being. By acknowledging and accepting change, seeking support, setting realistic expectations, practicing self-care, fostering a growth mindset, and embracing adaptability, individuals can navigate personal life changes with greater ease and find new paths to fulfillment and happiness.

Problem-Solving and Decision-Making Skills

Enhancing Problem-Solving Skills for Adaptability:

- ✓ Analytical Thinking: Develop analytical thinking skills to effectively assess and understand complex problems. Break down the problem into smaller components, gather relevant information, and analyze it systematically. Identify patterns, connections, and potential solutions.
  For example, if a business is experiencing declining sales, an individual with strong analytical thinking skills would gather sales data, analyze market trends, and identify potential factors contributing to the decline.
- ✓ Creative Thinking: Cultivate creative thinking to generate innovative solutions. Think outside the box, challenge assumptions, and explore unconventional approaches. Embrace brainstorming techniques, mind mapping, or other creative exercises to stimulate fresh ideas.
  For instance, when faced with a challenging project deadline, a team leader encourages team members to brainstorm creative solutions, such as utilizing new technologies or collaborating with external partners to expedite the process.

Effective Decision-Making in Uncertain Situations:

- ✓ Gather Information: Collect relevant data and information to make informed decisions. Seek multiple perspectives and diverse viewpoints to gain a comprehensive understanding of the situation. Utilize reliable sources, conduct research, and engage in discussions to gather valuable insights.

  For example, when deciding whether to invest in a new business venture, a savvy entrepreneur would gather market research, financial data, and consult industry experts to make an informed decision.
- ✓ Assess Risks and Benefits: Evaluate the risks and benefits associated with each decision. Consider potential outcomes, probabilities, and potential consequences. Assess the potential impact on stakeholders, resources, and long-term goals. Strive for a balance between taking calculated risks and maximizing rewards.

  For instance, when considering a job offer in a different city, an individual would assess the risks of relocating, such as uprooting their family or leaving behind a supportive network, alongside the potential benefits, such as career advancement opportunities or a higher salary.

Balancing Risks and Rewards:

- ✓ Weigh Alternatives: Consider multiple alternatives and evaluate their respective risks and rewards. Assess the feasibility, potential outcomes, and alignment with goals. Compare the trade-offs and make a decision that offers the best balance between risks and rewards.

For example, a business owner deciding on a marketing strategy may consider various alternatives, such as investing in traditional advertising or exploring digital marketing channels. They would assess the risks and rewards of each option before making a decision.

- ✓ Seek Input and Collaboration: Engage in collaborative decision-making by seeking input from stakeholders, colleagues, or subject matter experts. Embrace diverse perspectives and leverage the collective wisdom to identify potential risks and opportunities. Collaborative decision-making enhances the quality of decisions and reduces blind spots.

  For instance, when a project team needs to choose a software development framework, they may hold meetings to gather input from team members with different expertise and backgrounds. The collaborative process helps identify potential risks and select the most suitable framework.

In summary, enhancing problem-solving skills and effective decision-making is crucial for adaptability. By developing analytical and creative thinking, gathering relevant information, assessing risks and benefits, and balancing risks and rewards, individuals can make informed decisions in uncertain situations. With strong problem-solving and decision-making abilities, individuals can navigate challenges, seize opportunities, and adapt to ever-changing circumstances.

Building a Supportive Network

The Importance of a Support System During Challenging Times:

- ✓ Emotional Support: A support system plays a crucial role in providing emotional support during challenging times. It offers a safe space to express feelings, share concerns, and seek comfort. Knowing that there are people who genuinely care and understand can help individuals navigate through difficult situations with resilience.

  For example, during a period of personal loss, having friends or family members who offer a listening ear, empathy, and encouragement can provide solace and strength.
- ✓ Practical Assistance: A supportive network can also provide practical assistance when facing challenges. They can offer help with tasks, share resources, or provide guidance based on their own experiences. This practical support can alleviate the burden and facilitate problem-solving.

  For instance, when starting a new business, having a supportive network of entrepreneurs who can offer advice, connect with potential clients, or recommend valuable resources can significantly contribute to success.

Cultivating Relationships that Foster Adaptability:

- ✓ Seek Diverse Perspectives: Cultivate relationships with individuals from diverse backgrounds, professions, and experiences.

Engaging with people who have different perspectives broadens one's own worldview and encourages adaptability. Learning from diverse perspectives can help individuals approach challenges with fresh insights and open-mindedness.

For example, participating in networking events, joining professional associations, or engaging in online communities allows individuals to connect with people from various industries and backgrounds, fostering adaptability through exposure to different ideas and approaches.

- ✓ Foster Collaborative Relationships: Building collaborative relationships is essential for adaptability. Collaborating with others promotes teamwork, innovation, and collective problem-solving. By nurturing relationships based on trust, respect, and shared goals, individuals can leverage the strengths and expertise of others to adapt to changing circumstances.

  For instance, forming partnerships with colleagues or industry peers to tackle shared challenges or explore new opportunities enables individuals to pool resources, share knowledge, and adapt more effectively.

Seeking Mentorship and Guidance:

- ✓ Mentors: Seek mentors who have expertise in areas relevant to your personal or professional growth. A mentor can provide guidance, share their experiences, and offer valuable insights. Their wisdom and support can help individuals navigate challenges, overcome obstacles, and develop their adaptability skills.

For example, a young entrepreneur seeking to launch a startup may benefit from having a seasoned entrepreneur as a mentor who can provide guidance on business strategies, decision-making, and adapting to market changes.

- ✓ Coaches: Engage with coaches who specialize in personal or professional development. Coaches can provide support, accountability, and guidance in setting and achieving goals. They help individuals uncover their strengths, overcome limitations, and develop strategies for adaptability.

  For instance, a professional seeking to enhance their leadership skills may work with an executive coach who helps them identify areas for growth, develop adaptive strategies, and navigate complex work environments.

In summary, building a supportive network is crucial for adaptability. A strong support system provides emotional support and practical assistance during challenging times. Cultivating relationships with diverse perspectives and fostering collaborative connections enhances adaptability. Seeking mentorship and guidance from mentors or coaches provides valuable insights and support for personal and professional growth. By building a supportive network, individuals can navigate challenges, embrace change, and thrive in an ever-evolving world.

Harnessing Innovation to Adapt to New Challenges

Embrace Change and Disruption: Innovation involves embracing change and seeing it as an opportunity rather than a threat. Recognize that change is inevitable and actively seek ways to adapt and innovate in response to new challenges. By embracing innovation, individuals can stay ahead of the curve and navigate uncertainties with agility.
For example, a retail business facing declining foot traffic can embrace e-commerce and innovative digital marketing strategies to reach a wider audience and adapt to changing consumer behaviors.

Embrace Technology: Technology plays a vital role in driving innovation and adaptability. Embrace emerging technologies and explore how they can be integrated into your personal or professional life. Leverage digital tools, automation, artificial intelligence, and data analytics to streamline processes, enhance productivity, and find innovative solutions.
For instance, a healthcare provider can adopt telemedicine technologies to provide remote consultations, expanding their reach and adaptability to meet patients' changing needs.

Cultivating Creativity for Out-of-the-Box Solutions:

- ✓ Encourage a Creative Environment: Foster an environment that encourages creativity and fosters innovative thinking. Create spaces where ideas can be freely shared and encourage brainstorming sessions. Emphasize the value of diverse perspectives and encourage risk-taking and experimentation.

For example, companies like Google and Pixar have implemented innovative work environments that promote collaboration, creativity, and out-of-the-box thinking.

- ✓ Practice Divergent Thinking: Cultivate the ability to think divergently by exploring multiple possibilities and challenging assumptions. Allow yourself to think beyond conventional boundaries and explore alternative perspectives and ideas. This approach opens up new avenues for problem-solving and encourages innovative solutions.

  For instance, when faced with a supply chain disruption, a business can encourage employees to think divergently and explore unconventional sourcing options or creative production methods to adapt to the situation.

The Role of Experimentation and Iteration in Adaptability:

- ✓ Embrace a Growth Mindset: Adopt a growth mindset that values learning and improvement. Embrace the idea that failure is an opportunity to learn and iterate. Encourage experimentation and view setbacks as stepping stones to success. Embracing a growth mindset enables individuals to adapt to new challenges and find innovative solutions through continuous learning and improvement.

  For example, companies like Amazon are known for their culture of experimentation, where they encourage employees to take risks, learn from failures, and iterate their products and services based on customer feedback.

- ✓ Test and Learn: Embrace a test-and-learn approach to adaptability. Break down complex problems into smaller, manageable experiments. Test different ideas, solutions, or approaches, gather feedback, and iterate based on the results. This iterative process allows for continuous improvement and adaptability in the face of uncertainty.

  For instance, in product development, companies often release minimum viable products (MVPs) to gather user feedback and iterate on features and functionalities based on user preferences and needs.

In summary, embracing innovation and creativity is crucial for adaptability. By harnessing innovation, individuals can proactively respond to new challenges and stay ahead of the curve. Cultivating creativity fosters out-of-the-box thinking and enables individuals to find unique solutions. Embracing experimentation and iteration promotes adaptability through continuous learning and improvement. By embracing innovation and creativity, individuals can thrive in dynamic and ever-changing environments

Overcoming Fear and Embracing Change

Understanding the Fear of Change and its Impact on Adaptability:

- ✓ Fear of the Unknown: Change often involves stepping into the unknown, which can trigger fear and uncertainty. The fear of change stems from the fear of failure, loss, or the discomfort of leaving one's comfort zone. This fear can hinder adaptability as individuals may resist or avoid change, limiting their growth and potential.
- ✓ Comfort Zone and Familiarity Bias: People tend to gravitate towards what is familiar and comfortable. This familiarity bias can create resistance to change, even when it may be necessary for personal or professional growth. The fear of stepping outside the comfort zone can prevent individuals from embracing new opportunities and adapting to change effectively.

Techniques for Managing Fear and Embracing Change:

- ✓ Awareness and Acceptance: Recognize and acknowledge your fear of change. Understand that fear is a natural response to the unknown. By accepting your fear, you can begin to take steps towards managing it and embracing change. Embrace the mindset that change presents opportunities for growth and learning.
- ✓ Reframe Perspectives: Challenge negative thoughts and beliefs associated with change.

Instead of focusing on potential risks or failures, reframe your perspective to see change as a chance for personal development and new experiences. Embrace a positive mindset and view change as a catalyst for growth and improvement.

- ✓ Gradual Exposure: Take small steps towards change to gradually build resilience and adaptability. Break down larger changes into manageable tasks or milestones. By gradually exposing yourself to new experiences, you can build confidence, overcome fear, and develop adaptability skills.
- ✓ Seek Support: Reach out to a supportive network of friends, family, or mentors who can provide guidance and encouragement. Sharing fears and concerns with trusted individuals can provide emotional support and practical advice, making the process of embracing change more manageable.

Celebrating the Rewards of Stepping Outside Your Comfort Zone:

- ✓ Personal Growth: Stepping outside your comfort zone and embracing change leads to personal growth and development. It allows you to acquire new skills, knowledge, and experiences that can enhance your adaptability and broaden your horizons. Embracing change enables you to discover your true potential and overcome self-imposed limitations.
- ✓ Increased Resilience: Overcoming fear and embracing change builds resilience. By navigating unfamiliar territory and adapting to

new circumstances, you become more resilient in the face of future challenges. Each experience of embracing change strengthens your ability to handle uncertainty and adapt effectively.

- ✓ Expanded Opportunities: Embracing change opens doors to new opportunities. By being open to change, you expose yourself to possibilities that may have been previously inaccessible. Stepping outside your comfort zone allows you to explore new paths, meet new people, and seize opportunities for personal and professional growth.
- ✓ Enhanced Creativity and Innovation: Embracing change stimulates creativity and innovation. By exposing yourself to new experiences and perspectives, you can generate fresh ideas and approaches. Stepping outside your comfort zone encourages thinking outside the box, leading to innovative solutions and adaptability in various aspects of life.

In summary, overcoming fear and embracing change is essential for adaptability. Understanding the fear of change and its impact on adaptability allows individuals to address and manage their fears effectively. Techniques such as awareness, reframing perspectives, gradual exposure, and seeking support help individuals navigate and embrace change. By stepping outside the comfort zone and celebrating the rewards of change, individuals can unlock personal growth, resilience, expanded opportunities, and enhanced creativity. Embracing change becomes a transformative journey that leads to increased adaptability and success in an ever-changing world.

Maintaining Adaptability in the Long Run

Strategies for Sustaining Adaptability Over Time:

- ✓ Embrace a Growth Mindset: Cultivate a growth mindset that thrives on learning, improvement, and adaptability. Embrace the belief that abilities and skills can be developed through dedication and effort. Continuously challenge yourself to step outside your comfort zone and embrace new opportunities for growth and adaptation.
- ✓ Stay Curious and Open-Minded: Maintain a sense of curiosity and a willingness to explore new ideas, perspectives, and experiences. Be open to learning from others and embracing diverse viewpoints. Curiosity fosters adaptability by encouraging a proactive approach to seeking knowledge and understanding.
- ✓ Set Meaningful Goals: Establish meaningful goals that align with your values and aspirations. Setting clear goals provides a sense of purpose and direction, guiding your efforts towards continuous growth and adaptability. Regularly assess and update your goals to reflect changing circumstances and evolving priorities.

The Importance of Continuous Self-Reflection and Improvement:

- ✓ Self-Reflection: Engage in regular self-reflection to assess your strengths, weaknesses, and areas for improvement.

Reflect on past experiences and identify lessons learned that can inform future decisions and actions. Self-reflection helps you develop self-awareness, enabling you to adapt and make necessary adjustments to your mindset and behaviors.

- ✓ Adaptability Assessments: Consider taking adaptability assessments or seeking feedback from trusted mentors, colleagues, or coaches. These assessments can provide valuable insights into your adaptability skills, highlighting areas that may need further development. Use this feedback as a guide to continuously enhance your adaptability.
- ✓ Continuous Improvement: Adopt a mindset of continuous improvement. Embrace feedback as an opportunity for growth and actively seek ways to enhance your skills and adaptability. Engage in regular self-assessment, identify areas of improvement, and develop action plans to address them. Continuously seek learning opportunities, whether through courses, workshops, or self-study, to expand your knowledge and skill set.

Embracing Lifelong Learning and Personal Growth:

- ✓ Pursue Learning Opportunities: Embrace a lifelong learning mindset by actively seeking out learning opportunities. Stay informed about industry trends, advancements, and emerging technologies. Attend conferences, workshops, and webinars to expand your knowledge and stay ahead of the curve. Engaging in continuous learning enhances your adaptability by equipping you with the necessary skills and knowledge to navigate changing environments.

- ✓ Develop New Skills: Identify key skills that are relevant to your personal and professional growth. Invest time and effort into developing those skills through formal education, online courses, or on-the-job training. Acquiring new skills expands your versatility and adaptability, enabling you to tackle new challenges and embrace changing circumstances.
- ✓ Embrace Personal Growth: Personal growth is closely intertwined with adaptability. Seek opportunities for personal development, such as engaging in hobbies, practicing mindfulness, or seeking personal coaching. These activities enhance self-awareness, emotional intelligence, and resilience, fostering adaptability in various aspects of life.

Examples:

- ✓ An individual working in the technology industry regularly attends conferences and workshops to stay updated on the latest advancements and trends. This commitment to lifelong learning ensures they remain adaptable and well-informed about emerging technologies, enabling them to adapt to industry changes.
- ✓ A manager actively seeks feedback from their team and participates in leadership development programs. Through self-reflection and continuous improvement, they identify areas for growth, such as improving communication skills or delegating

responsibilities. By embracing personal growth, they enhance their adaptability as a leader and create an environment that encourages growth and innovation.

- ✓ A professional in a rapidly evolving field dedicates time each week to learn new skills relevant to their industry. They take online courses, join industry forums, and engage in networking opportunities. By continuously expanding their skill set, they ensure they remain adaptable and marketable, ready to embrace new opportunities and challenges.

In summary, maintaining adaptability in the long run requires strategies such as embracing a growth mindset, staying curious and open-minded, and setting meaningful goals. Continuous self-reflection and improvement play a crucial role, allowing individuals to assess their adaptability and make necessary adjustments. Embracing lifelong learning and personal growth ensures individuals stay equipped with the skills and knowledge needed to navigate changing environments. By implementing these strategies and examples, individuals can sustain adaptability and thrive in an ever-changing world.

30 Powerful Quotes on Adaptability

Here is a list of 30 powerful quotes by famous personalities on adaptability:

1. *"It is not the strongest of the species that survives, nor the most intelligent that survives. It is the one that is most adaptable to change." - Charles Darwin*
2. *"The measure of intelligence is the ability to change." - Albert Einstein*
3. *"Adaptability is not imitation. It means power of resistance and assimilation." - Mahatma Gandhi*
4. *"The art of life is a constant readjustment to our surroundings." - Kakuzo Okakura*
5. *"Adaptability is about the powerful difference between adapting to cope and adapting to win." - Max McKeown*
6. *"The only way to make sense out of change is to plunge into it, move with it, and join the dance." - Alan Watts*
7. *"The art of living lies less in eliminating our troubles than in growing with them." - Bernard M. Baruch*
8. *"Intelligence is the ability to adapt to change." - Stephen Hawking*
9. *"Life is 10% what happens to us and 90% how we react to it." - Charles R. Swindoll*
10. *"Adaptability is being able to adjust to any situation at any given time." - John Wooden*
11. *"The greatest glory in living lies not in never falling, but in rising every time we fall." - Nelson Mandela*

12. *"Adaptability is not necessarily about change, but rather about the capacity to deal with change." - Al Johnson*
13. *"Adaptability is not imitation, it means power of resistance and assimilation." - Mahatma Gandhi*
14. *"It is not the strongest of the species that survives, nor the most intelligent, but the one most responsive to change." - Charles Darwin*
15. *"Adaptability is the simple secret of survival." - Jessica Hagedorn*
16. *"Adaptability is not something you possess, but rather something you demonstrate." - Bryant McGill*
17. *"The art of life is a constant readjustment to our surroundings." - Kakuzo Okakura*
18. *"The only way to make sense out of change is to plunge into it, move with it, and join the dance." - Alan Watts*
19. *"Adaptability is not about compromise. It's about finding new ways to achieve the same goals." - Brian Tracy*
20. *"Adaptability is the key to survival in the modern world." - Richard Branson*
21. *"Adaptability is being able to adjust to any situation at any given time." - John Wooden*
22. *"Adaptability is not about change, it's about how you respond to it." - Lou Holtz*
23. *"Adaptability is not imitation, it means power of resistance and assimilation." - Mahatma Gandhi*
24. *"The only way to make sense out of change is to plunge into it, move with it, and join the dance." - Alan Watts*

25. *"Adaptability is not something you possess, but rather something you demonstrate." - Bryant McGill*
26. *"Adaptability is not about compromise. It's about finding new ways to achieve the same goals." - Brian Tracy*
27. *"Adaptability is the key to survival in the modern world." - Richard Branson*
28. *"Adaptability is being able to adjust to any situation at any given time." - John Wooden*
29. *"Adaptability is not about change, it's about how you respond to it." - Lou Holtz*
30. *"The art of life is a constant readjustment to our surroundings." - Kakuzo Okakura*

Conclusion

Congratulations on completing **"Adaptability: *Key Skills to Rising & Shining During Changing & Unforeseen Challenges!*"** This book has been a comprehensive exploration of the essential skills and mindset required to navigate the ever-changing world we live in.

Throughout this journey, we have learned that adaptability is not just a desirable trait, but a necessary skill for personal and professional success. We have discovered the power of a growth mindset, resilience, emotional intelligence, flexibility, and continuous learning in embracing change and thriving in the face of uncertainty.

By understanding the psychology behind adaptability and developing these key skills, you have equipped yourself with the tools to rise above unforeseen challenges and seize opportunities for growth. You have learned how to navigate organizational changes, adapt to new roles and responsibilities, and thrive in dynamic work environments. Moreover, you have explored strategies for managing life transitions, embracing personal growth, and maintaining well-being during times of change.

The transformative power of adaptability is evident in the examples and stories shared throughout this book. From individuals who have successfully reinvented themselves to organizations that have embraced innovation and overcome adversity, we have witnessed the remarkable outcomes that arise from embracing adaptability.

As you close this book, remember that adaptability is a lifelong journey. The skills and insights gained here are meant to be practiced and refined continuously. The world will continue to change, and new challenges will arise. But armed with the knowledge and tools acquired, you are well-prepared to face whatever comes your way.

Embrace change with confidence, knowing that you possess the resilience, flexibility, and mindset necessary to navigate uncharted territories. See challenges as opportunities for growth and transformation. Surround yourself with a supportive network that uplifts and encourages your adaptability journey.

Remember, the power to rise and shine during changing and unforeseen challenges lies within you. Embrace the lessons learned from this book and let adaptability be your guiding light as you navigate the ever-evolving landscape of life.

May your journey be filled with continuous learning, personal growth, and the fulfillment that comes from embracing the transformative power of adaptability.

Wishing you success, resilience, and a future filled with shining moments in the face of change!

About the Author 'GERARD ASSEY'

Gerard Assey is a Graduate in Economics, a PGD in Management (HRD) and holds a Doctorate in Leadership. Gerard holds several International Qualifications in Sales, Debt Collection, Training & Teaching, and is a 'Fellow' of the prestigious 'Institute of Sales & Marketing Management'-UK, a Certified NLP Practitioner, a 'Certified Trainer', an 'Accredited Management Teacher-Behavioral Sciences', a 'Certified Competency Facilitator', a 'Certified Management Consultant'- (the International credentials of a professional management consultant, awarded in accordance with global standards of the ICMCI); and a Certification from the University of Michigan in 'Successful Negotiation: Essential Strategies and Skills'

He is also a Member of the 'National Association of Sales Professionals' backed with several years experience in varied industries, both in India and Overseas. He also holds an 'Etiquette Consultant' Certification from the USA (by Sue Fox, Author of Best Seller: 'Business Etiquette for Dummies'. She has trained some of the top celebrities' world over). He was also a recipient of a scholarship for extensive training in Japan on 'Corporate Management for India'.

Gerard Assey is 'Founder & Chief Corporate Trainer' of the Group: '**Citius, Altius, Fortius Unlimited**'- an organization that **celebrated 20 years of Glorious Service** in 2021, focusing on 3 Core Competencies:

People. Performance. Profit; in functional areas of Sales & Marketing, HR & Organizational Development, covering Recruitment, Training & Consultancy!

Having managed organizations with large Sales Forces in India & Overseas, his specialization cover extensive areas of Sales Training (All levels - Presentation, Negotiation, Key/ Strategic Accounts Management & Managerial Skills for all sectors), Bid Proposal/ Capture Planning/ Management Trainings, Retail Sales, Customer Service & Customer Retention Programs, Training for Prevention & Collection of Debt, Self & Personal Development Programs (Time Management, Teamwork & Team Building, Business Etiquette & Personal Grooming, Leadership & Managerial Skills, People Management Skills, Train-the-Trainer etc), including preparation of Custom-designed Business Manuals for Internal (HR, Induction, and Sales etc) & External use (Instruction, User Manuals).

Gerard has successfully conducted over 6150 Trainings & Workshops (as of April '24) all across India, Middle East, Africa, Europe & S.E. Asia. Besides public programs conducted regularly, both in India & Overseas, he has some of the top names as clients whom he services from Single Owners to large Public & Government undertakings, covering all sectors, for their in-house needs.

His website: www.CollectionSkills.com is the only one in this part of the world to be featured in the 'Collections & Credit Risk Magazine-USA' under 'Who's Who in Training' and ranks TOP, along with other websites listed below on most search engines.

Gerard is author of 126 books already (May 2024)

A few of our business related books:

1. Bite-sized Bits on Commonsense Management
2. Heart to Heart on Life's Principles'
3. How to become a Successful Manager
4. The Sales Professionals' Master Workbook of S.Y.S.T.E.M.S
5. The Professional Business Email Etiquette Handbook & Guide
6. The Professional Business Video-Conferencing Etiquette Handbook & Guide
7. Professional Presentation Skills
8. Exceptional Customer Service
9. Professional Tele-Marketing Skills
10. Professional Debt Collection Skills
11. The G.R.E.A.T. Sales & Service Workbook
12. Sales Training Advantage for Results (*The Ultimate Sales Training Manual to enable you stand out as a S.T.A.R.*)
13. CEO Daily Planner & Organizer
14. The Sales Professionals' Master Daily Planner
15. The Professional Debt Collector's Master Daily Planner
16. My Daily Planner & Organizer
17. MY EMERGENCY INFORMATION RECORD (Family Emergency & Peace of Mind Planner)
18. The Ultimate Therapist & Counselors Planner and Organizer
19. Building an Ethical Workplace
20. Managing Relationships at Work
21. Managing Business Meetings Effectively
22. Effective Delegation Skills
23. Goal Setting for Success
24. B2B Selling by Email
25. Professional Business Etiquette & Grooming
26. Dining Etiquette & Table Manners
27. Effective Networking Skills
28. Grooming, Etiquette & Manners for Teens, Young Adults & Future Leaders
29. Inter-Personal Skills
30. Get Ready, Get Hired!
31. Selling in a Recession
32. Effective Receivables Management in an Economic Downturn!
33. Real Estate & Property Sales Training

34. Credit Sales & Accounts Receivable Management
35. Selling Skills for Real Estate & Property Advisors
36. Take G.R.E.A.T. C.A.R.E!
37. Spa, Salon & Health Club Selling Skills
38. Selling Travel, Holiday & MICE Services
39. Selling Skills for Spa's, Salons & Health Clubs
40. Retailing in Salons & Spas
41. Selling Holiday, Vacation, Tours & Packages
42. The Power of Sales Referrals
43. Selling Luxury
44. Technical Selling Skills
45. Financial Advisors Sales Training
46. Dealing with Burnout at Work Monopolize Your Markets
47. Selling to Affluent Customers
48. Growing up with Grace
49. Financial Selling Skills
50. *The Effective Manager's Guide: Key Skills to Thrive*
51. From Aspiring to Inspiring: A Guide for New Managers on the Rise
52. The Power of Focus
53. Selling with Integrity: Sell Like Jesus The Perfect Role Model!
54. 31 Habits of Champions: Your 31-Day Journey to Greatness
55. Rejecting Grasshopper Talk: From Grasshopper to Giant-Killer-*Defeating Giants Daily!*
56. Navigate the AI-Powered Future of Bid & Proposals: Up-Skill to Stay Relevant with Alternative Career Paths & Opportunities
57. Hiring Sales Winners
58. Present with Impact
59. Success Unlocked: *Breaking Free from Habits that Hold You Back*
60. Complaints to Cheers, Feedback to Gold: Mastering Complaints Management
61. Thriving Together: *Cultivating Diversity, Equity, and Inclusion*
62. Coaching Skills for Sales Managers
63. Soaring to Success in Business & Leadership: Swifter, Higher, Stronger!
64. From Classroom to Podium: A Student's Guide to Powerful Public Speaking & Presentation Skills

65. Developing Self-Discipline
66. The CEO's 31-Day Power Plan: Unlocking Success through Essential Traits
67. Credibility Matters
68. A Winning Attitude
69. Bid & Proposal Management Using AI
70. Sales Forecasting: A Practical & Proven Guide to Strategic Sales Forecasting
71. Elevate & Energize: *50 Dynamic & Fun Activities for Peak Workplace Morale*
72. 'Sales SOS! Sales on Fire! *30 Days to Conquer Chaos & the Nightmares of Success!'*
73. Mastering Sales Managerial Skills: *Building High-Performing Teams & Driving Exceptional Results*
74. Eagle-Eyed Leadership: Unleashing the Power of 31 Lessons from Eagles
75. The Ultimate Employee Training Guide: *Training Today, Leading Tomorrow*
76. Being More Accountable at Work
77. Creating a Culture of Continuous Improvement
78. Effective Questioning & Listening Skills
79. The Power of Value Selling
80. The Growth Mindset
81. Mastering Professional Help Desk Skills
82. The Power to Lead with Empathy
83. Being Prepared: The Key to Unlocking Success
84. Youthful Spark-Youth Energizers, Activities and Games-Igniting the Fun in Youth
85. Ignite your Motivation for Success
86. Elevate Your Executive Presence: *Your Roadmap to Executive Excellence*
87. Smart Decisions: *Mastering Problem Solving with Strategic Solutions for Business Success*
88. Strategic Planning: *Developing and Implementing Strategic Plans to Achieve Long-Term Business Goals*
89. The Power of Stay Interviews
90. Developing G.R.I.T.
91. Adaptability

Besides regularly contributing to business & trade journals, including international ones such as the 'Creative Training Techniques' and the 'Sales News' of the U.S.A, He is also a member of several prestigious bodies & trade associations, having participated in many Conferences & Workshops in India & Overseas.

Prior to his last assignment of leading & managing a large MNC as head, Gerard had a 3-year stint in the Middle East as a Consultant with a leading British Consultancy Firm.

As the past 'Official Country Representative' for the International Business Award- 'THE STEVIES'-(the business world's own Oscar) for about 4 years- he ensured a few Indian companies that qualify for the same every year!

Gerard can be contacted at:
Email: training@Sales-Training.in,training@CollectionSkills.com
Websites:

www.Sales-Training.in
www.EtiquetteWorks.in
www.CollectionSkills.com
www.RetailSalesTraining.in
www.SalesTrainingIndia.com
www.ManualPreparation.com
www.TrainingWithPuppets.com
www.FirstContactAcademy.com
www.SalesAndMarketingRecruiter.com

Our TRAININGS that can help your team

- ✓ **Sales Effectiveness**: Selling Skills for any Sector: Service/ Logistics/ FMCG Realty/ Insurance & Finance/ Media/ SPA's, Health Clubs & Salons/ Key Account Management, Effective Negotiation Skills/ Bid & Proposal Management Skills/ Retail Sales Training: Any Sector (Auto, Jewelry, Clothing, Luxury etc)
- ✓ **Customer Service Skills**-Complaints Handling & Customer Retention
- ✓ **Debt Prevention & Collection Skills**
- ✓ **Etiquette & Grooming**
- ✓ **Leadership & Managerial Skills**
- ✓ **Self & Personal Development Skills**: Presentation Skills/ Effective Communication Skills/Business Proposal Writing Skills/ Problem Solving & Decision Making Skills/ Empowering Secretaries-The perfect PA! (For Secretaries & PA's)/ Effective Time Management/ Teamwork & Teambuilding/ P.R.I.D.E- **P**ersonal **R**esponsibility **I**n **D**elivering **E**xcellence

www.ingramcontent.com/pod-product-compliance
Lightning Source LLC
Chambersburg PA
CBHW062111160726
48282CB00026B/764
* 9 7 8 9 3 9 2 4 9 2 4 7 1 *